FAR-OUT and UNUSUAL

pets

IGUANAS

Cool Pets!

Enslow Elementary

an imprint of

Enslow Publishers, Inc.

40 Industrial Road
Box 398
Berkeley Heights, NJ 07922
USA

http://www.enslow.com

Alvin and Virginia
Silverstein and Laura
Silverstein Nunn

Enslow Elementary, an imprint of Enslow Publishers, Inc.

Enslow Elementary® is a registered trademark of Enslow Publishers, Inc.

Library of Congress Cataloging-in-Publication Data
Silverstein, Alvin.
 Iguanas : cool pets! / by Alvin Silverstein, Virginia Silverstein, and Laura Silverstein Nunn.
   p. cm. — (Far-out and unusual pets)
 Includes bibliographical references and index.
 Summary: "Provides basic information about iguanas and keeping them as pets"
—Provided by publisher.
 ISBN 978-0-7660-3686-4
 1. Iguanas as pets—Juvenile literature. I. Silverstein, Virginia B. II. Nunn, Laura Silverstein. III. Title.
 SF459.I38S55 2012
 639.3'9542—dc22
                              2010006292

Printed in the United States of America

092010 Lake Book Manufacturing, Inc., Melrose Park, IL

10 9 8 7 6 5 4 3 2 1

To Our Readers: We have done our best to make sure all Internet Addresses in this book were
active and appropriate when we went to press. However, the author and the publisher have no
control over and assume no liability for the material available on those Internet sites or on other Web
sites they may link to. Any comments or suggestions can be sent by e-mail to comments@enslow.com
or to the address on the back cover.

♻ Enslow Publishers, Inc., is committed to printing our books on recycled paper. The paper in
every book contains 10% to 30% post-consumer waste (PCW). The cover board on the outside
of each book contains 100% PCW. Our goal is to do our part to help young people and the
environment too!

Photo credits: © age fotostock/SuperStock, p. 18; Associated Press, pp. 5, 43; Courtesy Stephen
Pecoraro, pp. 16, 26; The Image Bank/Getty Images, p. 28; © iStockphoto.com: Andrey Parfenov,
pp. 1, 4, Craig Robinson, p. 6, Elena Casalegno, p. 24, Jana Lumley, p. 14, Lynne Barrows, p. 15,
Mehmet Salih Guler, p. 41, Niroot Sampan, p. 10, Patrick Roherty, p. 12, Roger de Montfort, p. 25;
Kenneth M. Highfill/Photo Researchers, Inc., p. 22; Ridolf Coertze, p. 33; Shutterstock.com, pp. 3,
8, 19, 20, 35, 37, 39.

Illustration credits: © 2010 Gerald Kelley, www.geraldkelley.com

Cover Photo: © iStockphoto.com/Andrey Parfenov (iguana); Shutterstock.com (hat).

Contents

The Gentle Giant

Have you ever watched any Godzilla movies? Godzilla looks like a scary dinosaur. It is a scaly reptile with long spikes down its back. Some people might even say Godzilla looks like an iguana.

An iguana is no scary beast, though. In fact, many people keep them as pets. Well-trained pet iguanas can be rather gentle. Their owners don't have to worry that their pet will eat them for lunch. Iguanas are plant eaters!

Some people say Godzilla looks like an iguana. But iguanas aren't scary monsters!

5

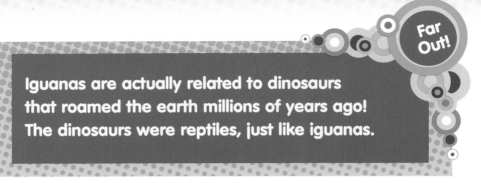

Iguanas are actually related to dinosaurs that roamed the earth millions of years ago! The dinosaurs were reptiles, just like iguanas.

Iguanas are the most popular reptile pets in the United States. What exactly are reptiles? And what makes them different from the typical pets people keep, such as cats and dogs? For one thing, reptiles don't have soft fur. Instead, they are covered in leathery scales.

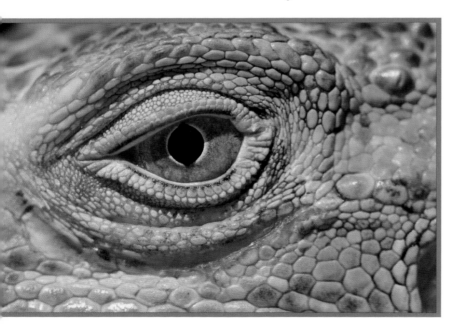

Iguanas, like all reptiles, are covered in scales.

Reptiles are also cold-blooded. That doesn't mean that their blood is always cold. It just means that their body temperature depends on the air around them. In cold places, they cool down. When it's hot, they heat up. Warm-blooded animals, such as cats, dogs, and you, can warm or cool their own bodies to stay comfortable.

Female reptiles lay eggs. (Cats and dogs can't do that!) Baby reptiles grow inside the eggs. Iguanas take five months to hatch. When they hatch, they look like tiny copies of their parents.

Reptiles include turtles, alligators, crocodiles, snakes, and lizards, such as the iguana.

The iguana is the biggest lizard people keep as pets. Adults may be as much as 5 to 6 feet (1.5 to 1.8 meters) long! But don't let their size scare you. If you go about it the right way, iguanas can be tamed. They can be trained to eat from your hand. They can also learn to come when you call their name.

You can train your iguana to come when called, or even to eat out of your hand.

Iguanas may be fun and interesting, but keeping them as pets is a big responsibility. It is very important to learn about iguanas and their needs before owning one. With the right care, your iguana can live for many years. Read on and find out what makes iguanas such far-out and unusual pets.

2

The First Iguana Pets

Iguanas have been kept as pets at least since the 1940s. Back then, it was not easy to find iguanas for sale.

Even if you were lucky enough to find an iguana for sale, no one seemed to know much about them. What kind of cage do they need? What do they eat? How do you keep them healthy? Too often, iguana pets did not live very long.

Coming to America

Wild iguanas are found mostly in the forests of southern Mexico, Central America, and South America. They spend a lot of time in trees.

Wild iguanas like to spend their time in trees.

These lizards are great climbers. They have very sharp, strong claws. The claws help them hold onto tree trunks and branches.

By the mid-1900s, many people wanted to own unusual pets. They were interested in something different from cats or dogs. In the 1950s and 1960s, large numbers of iguanas were taken from their homes in the wild. Many of them were baby iguanas, which were small and cute. Animal dealers brought many iguanas to America to sell.

Unfortunately, there were no iguana pet care books available. People still had no idea what to feed their pets to keep them healthy.

Did You Know?

Until the 1990s, most iguana pets died within a year or two. People thought this was just normal "old age" since very few survived much longer.

Mystery Solved

For years, scientists tried to figure out why iguana pets did not live very long. The mystery was not solved until the early 1980s. A book called *Iguanas of the World: Their Behavior, Ecology, and Conservation* was published in 1982. This book included iguana research by more than thirty scientists.

What did the researchers find out about iguanas? For one thing, they learned that these lizards are *not* meat eaters as many people believed. At the time, the typical diet for pet iguanas included insects, mice, cat food, dog food, chicken, and beef, as well as some plant foods.

Most lizards, like this chameleon, are meat eaters. People used to think iguanas would eat crickets like chameleons do, but a meat diet made iguanas sick.

The pets seemed to like these foods. In fact, some wild iguanas will gobble down a grasshopper or caterpillar if they find one. But iguanas are mainly plant eaters. Their bodies cannot handle "meaty" foods, such as insects, very well. Eating too much meat will make them sick.

After this important book came out, researchers began new studies of pet iguanas. They learned which kinds of foods were best. They found that a good vegetable diet can help keep pet iguanas healthy for twenty years or more.

By the late 1980s, iguanas had become popular pets. In some warm places, such as Central America, people raise iguanas on iguana farms. They sell the baby iguanas. Most baby iguanas are shipped to the United States. This means that pet iguanas today most likely come from an iguana farm. They were not taken from the wild.

As iguanas became more popular as pets, however, another problem developed. Many people who bought them didn't know what they

Iguanas like to eat fruits and vegetables. Eating these foods keeps them healthy.

were getting into. They didn't realize the cute little baby they took home would grow to several feet long! They didn't know how to handle such a giant lizard. Some people took their iguanas miles away from home and let them go. In warm places, many

Iguanas in Florida

Wild iguanas can now be found in southern Florida. But they don't really belong there. Many were once family pets. Some owners left their iguanas in canals and swamps. Other iguanas escaped from their owners' homes and wandered into nearby woods. Some got loose when houses or pet shops were damaged by hurricanes.

It is usually warm all year in southern Florida. Iguanas live very well in the wild there. They have no problems having babies. Now thousands of iguanas live in southern Florida. They are pests. They eat garden plants and poop in swimming pools.

Responsible pet owners know the correct way to raise a healthy iguana. This iguana is healthy and happy!

of the iguanas survived. But in colder places, the iguanas most likely died.

Soon people wrote books and pamphlets with the latest information. They included many things a pet owner needs to know to raise a healthy iguana. Iguana owners can also find a lot of useful information on the Internet.

3

Do You Wanna Iguana?

How cool would it be to own an iguana? A newly hatched iguana is so small and cute. It is just 7 inches (18 cm) long, and most of that is the tail.

A baby iguana is small enough to hold in the palm of your hand. But in three to four years, your cute little iguana will grow to about 5 to 6 feet (1.5 to 1.8 meters)! More than half of that is the tail.

Iguanas are pretty cool, no matter what their size. But a full-size iguana is a lot to handle. Let's take a closer look at this lizard and see if it is the right pet for you.

This iguana is hatching from its egg. A baby iguana would fit in the palm of your hand.

The Iguana Close Up

The iguanas usually sold as pets are a kind called the green iguana. But not all green iguanas are green. Healthy young iguanas are bright green or bluish green. As they become adults, they may turn a dull green, gray, or brown. Some may even be

Iguanas can have many different colors and patterns.

orange with brown or black markings. Males are generally larger and more brightly colored than females.

An iguana's body is covered with rough, scaly skin. It has tooth-like spines on its back, from the neck down to its tail. An iguana also has a dewlap.

A dewlap is the flap of skin that hangs down from an iguana's neck. Male iguanas have bigger dewlaps than females.

This is a fold of skin hanging from its neck. Males typically have a much larger dewlap than females. They can spread the dewlap out as a warning to other males to "come no closer." Males may also show off their large dewlaps when they are trying to attract a mate.

Far Out!

A Third Eye?

Iguanas have a "third eye" on top of their head. It's not a complete eye. It can't see pictures. But it can tell when there are changes in light and darkness. In the wild, iguanas use their third eye to spot birds that swoop down to grab them for dinner. With this warning, the iguana can make a quick escape.

Where Do You Buy an Iguana?

Before you buy an iguana, make sure they are allowed as pets where you live. Some towns have laws against keeping these kinds of animals.

Iguanas are generally sold as pets at about one to three months of age. You can buy them in many pet stores. You can also get them from iguana rescue organizations. Reptile societies can give you a list of iguana breeders. It's smart to buy from someone who knows a lot about iguanas. They can answer any questions you might have.

Should you get more than one iguana? Will it get lonely if it's all by itself? Young iguanas may get along well with each other. But when they become adults, they may fight. Males are especially likely to fight to protect their territory. In the wild, their territory is the area where they live and get food. When an iguana is a pet, it will think of its cage— or even the whole house—as its territory. So it's best to keep just one iguana to avoid fighting. Pet iguanas do perfectly fine on their own.

Far Out!

Alone Time

In the wild, iguanas are often found in groups. They gather together to soak in the sun, to take a nap, or to snack on their favorite plants. But they are not really social animals the same way dogs or house cats are. They would rather spend some time alone. That doesn't mean you should lock your pet away in a garage. Iguanas do best when their cage is in a place where they can see and hear people. Having a window to look out is also helpful.

Getting a Handle on Iguanas

An iguana is not exactly soft and cuddly like a cat or dog. If you pick one up, you'll notice that the lizard's rough, scaly skin feels like sandpaper. And sometimes holding onto an iguana—even a little one—can be painful. The iguana may be nervous about being held. It might squirm around in your hands, digging its pointy spikes into your skin. If it gets really upset, it may nip you with its tiny, razor-sharp teeth. Ouch!

An iguana has sharp teeth.

Even though iguanas eat mostly plants, their teeth and claws are very sharp. Some people wear gloves when handling their pet.

As the iguana gets bigger, handling your pet becomes more of a challenge. It's not that it gets too heavy to lift. A full-grown iguana weighs only about 15 to 20 pounds (7 to 9 kg). But when you pick up one of this size, it may hold on by digging its sharp claws into your skin. And watch out if it starts to whip its long, spiky tail back and forth. If that tail hits you, it can really hurt.

Many lizards can drop off part of their tail as a trick for escaping danger. The enemy is left holding a wiggling tail while the lizard runs away. Eventually, the tail grows back. However, regrowing a tail is very stressful for iguanas, especially for the adults. If and when the tail does grow back, it may not be as long as the original tail. It may even be a different color or pattern.

Be very gentle when you hold your iguana. If your iguana is relaxed, its tail will hang down loosely.

In the wild, an iguana will defend itself by whipping its tail at its enemy. You need to move slowly and be very gentle when handling iguanas. Hold the iguana with its belly resting on your palm. The head should be looking between your fingers. The tail should be hanging down alongside your wrist. A relaxed iguana will let its legs hang down loosely.

Sometimes people let their iguana sit on their shoulder. But that's not a good idea. If the iguana gets nervous, it could whip its tail back and forth, right into its owner's face! It might even climb on top of the person's head. Not only is the tail a problem, but watch out for its claws. The iguana will be unsteady. It may try to grab onto the person's head or face with its sharp claws. That could really hurt!

4

Caring for an Iguana

Just like any pet, an iguana can become a part of the family. It may not be as easy as keeping a cat or dog, though. An iguana needs special care. You need to set up its home much like its home in the wild. It will take a lot of work to keep your iguana healthy and happy.

It is especially important to spend lots of time with your pet. With good training, your iguana will learn to trust you. Many pet owners say that their iguanas like having their bellies rubbed and their backs petted or scratched. Be patient, though. This may not happen for up to a year.

Handle With Care

Many iguanas carry a germ that can make people sick. It is a type of bacteria called salmonella. Bacteria from their droppings get on their skin and cages. Dust from the cages can even get into the air. So always wash your hands thoroughly after handling your iguana pet or touching anything in its cage.

A Home for Your Iguana

Young iguanas can be kept in a 50- to 60-gallon tank. As the iguana grows, though, it will need a much bigger cage. (A baby iguana will more than double its size in the first year!) A full-grown adult will need a cage at least 8 feet (2.4 meters) wide, 6 feet (1.8 meters) high, and 4 feet (1.2 meters) deep. You can't find a cage this big in a store. Your family will have to have one specially built.

Iguanas are tropical animals. That means they need to live in a warm, humid place. (Humidity is the amount of moisture in the air. In the tropics, the humidity is very high.) Remember that your pet is cold-blooded. It can't keep its body warm enough in a cold place. That is why reptiles often bask in the sun—to warm up. If they do not get the warmth they need, they may get sick or even die.

Iguanas need bigger cages as they grow older. Make sure your iguana's home is big enough for it to live comfortably.

Choosing Cages

What kind of cage should you choose for an adult iguana? Some people use a wire screen cage with a wood frame. But a wire cage doesn't hold in heat very well. It doesn't really keep in moisture, either. A better choice may be a cage with walls of glass or clear plastic. The solid walls will hold in the heat and moisture. That will help give it a tropical feel. With either kind of cage, use old newspapers to cover the floor. You can just throw them away when they get dirty.

So you need to keep an iguana's cage warm and humid. It should be at least 75°F (24°C). In most parts of the world, pet iguanas need an indoor cage with a heat lamp. There should also be a branch or shelf near the lamp. The temperature may be up to 95°F (35°C) there. The iguana will use this shelf for basking. But make sure the bulb is not too close to your pet. Touching a heat lamp could give an iguana a bad burn.

Set up a heat lamp
for your iguana.

The iguana cage also needs another kind of heater. That's because you need to turn the lights off at night. (Remember, you are trying to make your pet's home like the iguana's natural home in the tropics. It gets dark and a little cooler there when the sun goes down.)

In addition to heat, an iguana needs the right lighting to stay healthy. Bright lightbulbs can give both light and heat. Do not use the ordinary bulbs people use in lamps. There are special bulbs sold in pet stores. They include UV (ultraviolet) light. (That's the kind that's in sunlight and can give you a tan or sunburn.) There are two types of UV light that iguanas need: UV-A and UV-B. Ordinary lightbulbs don't give the UV light that iguanas need.

In the wild, iguanas spend a lot of time climbing in trees. So your iguana cage should have sturdy branches for climbing. Perches for resting high above the cage floor will also help your pet feel at home.

My Iguana Is Peeling!

Far Out!

From time to time, you may find pieces of skin peeling off your pet iguana. Don't worry—it's not sick. As an iguana grows, its tough, scaly skin can't grow with it. New skin forms underneath, and patches of old skin peel off. Giving your pet regular baths will help keep its skin healthy.

Humidity is also very important to an iguana's home. Use a spray bottle to mist the iguana's cage several times every day.

In the wild, iguanas spend some time in rivers and streams. They also like to bathe in shallow water. So your pet will need a large pan of water it can sit in. (It may also poop and pee there, too. You'll need to change that water often!)

What Do You Feed Your Iguana?

Your iguana should have a good mix of plant foods. You can feed it leaves and flowers, as well as torn-up collard, mustard, and dandelion greens. Shredded winter squash (including pumpkins), parsnips, and chopped green beans are also

Far Out!

In the wild, iguanas are great swimmers. Their powerful tail gives them a boost through the water. They can also stay underwater for up to forty minutes!

good iguana foods. You can add small amounts of zucchini, carrots, and romaine lettuce for variety. Shredded apple and pear are good, too. Use cut-up grapes, strawberries, and bananas for special treats.

There should also be a shallow water bowl. An iguana doesn't drink a lot. It gets most of its

Make sure your iguana gets a variety of fruits and vegetables to eat.

water from the fresh leaves that it eats. But it will take a sip once in a while. You can also spray its food with water.

Feed your iguana every day. How much and how many times a day depends on your iguana. A larger iguana may need to eat more often than a smaller one. Watch your iguana's eating habits for a few days. That will give you an idea of how much your pet likes to eat. (If it always leaves some food, you're giving it too much. If it eats every bit, you may need to feed it more.) It's a good idea to remove leftover food each night. That way, the food won't go bad.

Training Your Iguana

Iguanas are usually shy animals. You must be very gentle when handling them. To tame an iguana, you have to make it feel safe. When you reach into its cage, move slowly and smoothly. *Never* try to grab it from above! It may think you are a bird swooping down to eat it.

It may take your iguana some time to get used to being picked up.

Like people, iguanas are not all the same. Some like being handled; others do not. And if an iguana doesn't want to do something, it won't. But treats can help train your pet. You have to be *very* patient. And keep working to get your iguana used to being petted and picked up. There will be times—like trips to the vet—when you'll need to be able to pick it up without getting slapped by its tail or scratched by its claws.

Owners have trained iguanas to eat out of their hand. Iguanas can even be trained to "go potty" in only one part of the cage. Your iguana can also learn to understand words—for example, its own name. If you repeat everything, you can teach your pet everyday commands. "Come on," "Let's go for a ride," "Go take a bath," and "Go to your cage" are very useful.

Iguanas should not be kept in a cage all the time. Visits to different rooms in the house or

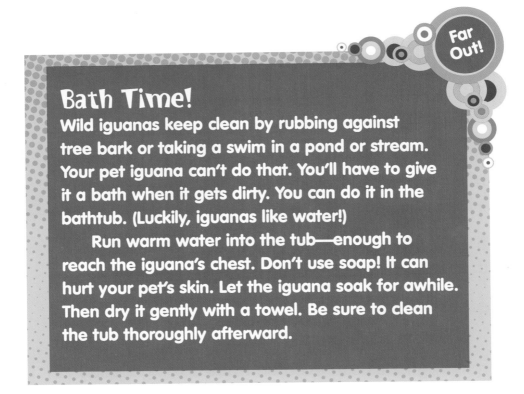

Bath Time!

Wild iguanas keep clean by rubbing against tree bark or taking a swim in a pond or stream. Your pet iguana can't do that. You'll have to give it a bath when it gets dirty. You can do it in the bathtub. (Luckily, iguanas like water!)

Run warm water into the tub—enough to reach the iguana's chest. Don't use soap! It can hurt your pet's skin. Let the iguana soak for awhile. Then dry it gently with a towel. Be sure to clean the tub thoroughly afterward.

outdoors on warm days help make their life more interesting.

Some people let their iguanas run loose in the house. But it's a good idea to keep an eye on your pet when it's out of its cage. An iguana left by itself could get hurt. And finding it later could be a

Your iguana will appreciate having new places to explore safely.

problem. You'd be surprised where a little iguana can hide.

In the wild, when an iguana feels threatened, it tries to get away from the threat as quickly as possible. It may climb farther up the tree it's in.

Or it may take its enemy by surprise and suddenly drop from a tree branch. An iguana lands on its feet, the way a cat does. It can drop 50 feet (more than 15 meters) without getting hurt! As soon as it hits the ground, it quickly rushes off for cover.

In your home, an iguana will still act as it would in nature. It may try to climb anything in the room. That could be things that are pretty high, such as a curtain rod, the top of a bookcase, or even your head! Then without warning, it may suddenly drop down to the floor. That would seem natural in the wild. But it can look pretty funny when it happens in your living room.

Iguanas are cool and different. But would one make a great pet for you and your family? An iguana will not turn into a dream pet overnight. It takes a lot of hard work. It can also cost a lot of money. Find out what you're getting into first. Remember, your pet will be a part of your family for twenty years or more!

Words to Know

bacteria—A kind of germ; some bacteria cause illness.

bask—To lie in a warm spot.

breed—To mate animals and raise their young.

cold-blooded—Describes an animal with a body temperature that warms up in warm air and cools down in cool air.

dewlap—A flap of skin hanging on an animal's neck.

humidity—The amount of moisture in the air.

reptile—A cold-blooded, egg-laying animal covered with scales or plates.

salmonella—A kind of bacterium that causes food poisoning.

territory—The area where an animal lives and gets its food. Some animals will defend their home territory against others of their own kind.

tropical—Describes places that are warm or hot all year round.

UV (ultraviolet) light—Part of the light energy given off by the sun.

warm-blooded—Describes an animal with a body temperature that stays fairly constant.

Learn More

Books

Landau, Elaine. *Your Pet Iguana*. New York: Children's Press, 2007.

Lunis, Natalie. *Green Iguanas*. New York: Bearport Publishing Company, Inc., 2010.

Velthaus, Sally. *Green Iguanas*. Mankato, Minn.: Capstone Press, 2006.

Web Sites

Green Iguana Society Kids Club
<http://www.greenigsociety.org/kidsclub>

Pet Iguana Care
<http://www.petiguanacare.com/>

San Diego Zoo
<http://sandiegozoo.org/animalbytes/t-iguana.html>

Index